basic
seed
saving

**Easy step by step instructions
for 18 vegetables and 29 wildflowers**

by Bill McDorman

I would like to thank Cary Fowler for his inspiration, Wes McDorman for his encouragement, Teri Dunn and Stephen Thomas for their editing skills and Belle for her unending support. Any remaining mistakes are my responsibility.

3rd Edition

ISBN (978-0-615-33231-4)

Printed in United States of America

Published by
Higher Ground, LLC
PO Box 596, Cornville, AZ 86325
belle@seedsave.org

TABLE OF CONTENTS

CHAPTER I

INTRODUCTION

Every time you purchase seeds, you miss out on one of nature's most magical opportunities. Saving and replanting seeds allows you to carry the best of your garden's harvest into the next season—and the next, and the next. This incredible potential for adaptability is unparalleled in our modern technology. Miraculously, seeds have the power to self-replicate. They contain the software and hardware necessary to evolve in real-time based on information from the environment.

With a curious gardener behind this process, our saved seeds can change and adapt season after season to our immediate wants and needs. Flavors, colors, and traits grow more prominent and refined. But when we buy seeds, we start from scratch. We break the cycle and ignore this remarkable potential.

For more than 300 generations, we humans have been saving the seeds from the plants we favor, replanting them again and again in an elegant ritual. Food crops that now feed the world's population arose this way, developed over millennia from wild plants. This practice emerged naturally, instinctively, and well before the science of modern plant genetics was discovered.

Every ancient culture saved seeds. We are all the descendants of ingenious, inspired seed stewards who created an unimaginable display of diversity. This bounty is our sustenance and our birthright. But with the rise of industrial agriculture, the age-old cycle of seed saving has been shattered. An estimated 90% or more of the unique and nuanced seed varieties once available have disappeared from widespread use. And along with the seeds, an irreplaceable treasure of stories, traditions, and practical knowledge has been lost. This is tragic—but we can turn the tide.

The goal of Basic Seed Saving is to empower modern gardeners to begin saving their own seeds. It is organized to help everyone start with the easiest-to-save vegetables. My hope is that you will gain confidence from what you learn and move on through the book to the more complex varieties and procedures. Too many times I have seen new seed saving students get lost or discouraged by a barrage of complex concepts at the beginning of a seed saving book or workshop. Remember, detailed lessons in biology and genetics are only necessary for seed growers at the

industrial and market breeder levels. Home gardeners can afford to be playful and make "mistakes." In fact, many of the world's favorite crops are the result of small farmers and gardeners playfully experimenting with the resulting surprises found in their own fields and backyards.
        Start with the easy varieties. Have fun! And let yourself become inspired. If you give this process a chance, I am confident the seeds themselves will lead you deeper down the path into the magical world of seed saving.

THE REWARDS OF SEED SAVING

        With little more work than it takes to grow a home garden, we can together begin to re-elevate the gardening experience to a new, more sustainable, if not magical level. I experienced this first hand on my adventure to Siberia in 1989. I discovered millions of gardeners from all walks of life saving their own seeds. Seed saving was integral to the gardening experience, even in the busiest cities. Competition among Siberians for the "earliest and best tasting" was most intense. Surprisingly, the best results we observed came from **individuals saving their own seeds**. Siberian mail order catalogs did not yet exist. Packeted seeds were rare.
        Siberians tapped into real rewards for themselves and future generations by saving seeds from the plants they liked. I estimated at the time more than two million Siberian gardeners picking their own fresh tomatoes and saving the seeds. These gardeners, living behind the Iron Curtain, were largely cut off from access to modern Western varieties. Left with their own seeds and seed saving, they produced what many call now the world's best tasting tomatoes.
        The most inspiring part of my journey was learning that Siberians knew this was important, and that they wanted to share. I met a man in Irkutsk, Sasha, who walked 35 kilometers to his home and back in the Altai Mountains just to bring me seeds for what he called "best tasting tomato in Siberia". I was able to bring a few of his seeds home in my front pocket. I grew them, shared with Seed Savers Exchange, and sold them through my little seed company, High Altitude Gardens. I named the tomato *Sasha's Altai*. To this day, you can find *Sasha's Altai* listed as one of the earliest and best tasting tomatoes in dozens of seed catalogs around the world.
        I have a vision. Hundreds of years in the future, busy modern creatures eating mouth-watering tomatoes from their own urban gardens will raise a toast to us, the seed savers of the late 20th and early 21st centuries. They will thank us because we got the most important message of our day. Losing 90% of the diversity gifted to us was not OK. Diversity is necessary for the long-term health and sustainability of ecosystems. And most importantly, diversity makes our lives **better**. The easiest, cheapest, most efficient way to create and maintain agricultural diversity is to have everyone save their own seeds. I hope you too will rejoin this beautiful and life sustaining ritual. Bill McDorman, May 4, 2016.

CHAPTER II

BASIC TERMS

Basic Seed Saving was designed to limit the need for complicated genetic terms. The following terms provide a basic understanding of seeds and seed production.

Seeds are living, hibernating embryos. They have a life span and survive longest if kept cool, dark and dry.

Flowers are the portions of plants where reproduction takes place and seeds are produced.

Pistils are the female reproductive organs in flowers made up of the stigma, style and ovary. The stigma is the opening in the pistil through which the pollen passes on its way to the ovary. The style contains the pollen tube between the stigma and the ovary through which the pollen is carried. The ovary contains ovules. When fertilized, ovules develope into mature seeds.

Stamens are the male reproductive organs in flowers. They consist of the filament, anther and pollen. A filament is the tube that supports the anther where pollen is produced. Pollen is the equivalent of sperm. Pollen grains fertilize plant ovules.

Pollination is the process of sexual fertilization in plants. The different methods a flower uses for pollination will dictate the spacing or isolation necessary for plants to produce dependable seeds.

Self-pollination occurs without need for other flowers or plants because it takes place within the flower before it opens. Isolation distance to prevent cross-pollination is not necessary unless insects invade the flowers.

Perfect flowers contain the stamens which produce pollen and the pistil which receives the pollen. Some self-pollinate. Others are self-incompatible, meaning they will not receive their own pollen.

Cross-pollination takes place when pollen is exchanged between different flowers on the same or different plants. If not prevented, unwanted characteristics and traits may result in the offspring.

Isolation distance to prevent unwanted cross-pollination is the distance between two different flowers necessary to prevent pollen from being exchanged. Wind pollination is pollen exchange caused by wind and insect pollination is pollen exchange caused by insects, primarily bees.

Hybrids, the modern definition, are uniform varieties resulting from controlled pollination between distinct (inbred) parents. F1 (filial 1) is the 1st generation offspring after pollination. F2 hybrids (seed saved from F1's) lack the consistency of F1's, but usually retain desirable traits that can be further selected.

Open-pollinated varieties are stable varieties resulting from the pollination between the same or genetically similar parents. Not hybrid.

Monecious plants produce single plants with separate male flowers and female flowers on the same plant.

Dioecious plants produce separate male flowers and female flowers on different plants.

VEGETABLE SEED HEADINGS

The information provided for each individual vegetable is organized under the following bold-faced headings. The following section explains terms that may be encountered under each heading.

PLANT: The separation distance between plants necessary for successful seed production is given under this heading for each vegetable. Techniques to prevent cross-pollination other than by separation distance are also suggested.

Caging is a separation technique where insects that might cause cross-pollination are prevented from reaching flowers by a fine net supported by wire or wood. If flowers in the cage are not self-pollinating, several plants must be included in the cage and pollinating insects introduced. Alternate day caging allows two plants or two groups of plants to be naturally pollinated by insects. Unwanted cross-pollination is prevented because one plant or group of plants is caged one day and the other plant or group is caged the next.

Root to seed describes a technique used to produce seed for biennial crops. The roots of the biennials are harvested in the fall, trimmed and stored for the winter. The following spring, the best roots are planted for seed production that season. When roots to biennials are left in the ground in the fall to produce seeds the following summer, the term seed to seed is used.

FLOWER: A complete description of each vegetable's flower type and pollination method is given.

INBREEDING DEPRESSION: This section alerts gardeners to the possibility of a loss of vigor because of inbreeding. Vigor is a desirable characteristic that describes strong, vibrant germination and plant growth. Inbreeding can result from self-pollination or pollination between a small number of close relatives. Self-pollinating plants (selfers) show little sign of inbreeding depression even when self-pollinated for many generations, while cross-pollinating plants (crossers) can show signs of inbreeding depression even in the first generation offspring.

SELECTION: In the interest of clarity we make a distinction between selection characteristics and selection traits.

<u>Characteristics</u> are general features attributed to unidentified complexes of genes. Complex and hard to define, characteristics are often ignored by commercial breeders and offer the most rewards for home gardeners. Characteristics on my priority list include but are not limited to beauty, freeze tolerance, cold tolerance, heat tolerance, UV resistance, winter hardiness, early maturation, vigor, flavor and most recently the color purple. Every home gardener should create his or her own list of favorite selection characteristics.

<u>Traits</u> are specific features traceable to identifiable genes. For example, pea traits traceable to single genes include vine growth (bush or tall), seed texture (smooth or wrinkled) and disease resistance (fusarium, mosaic and powdery mildew).

<u>Dominant trait</u>, abbreviated "D", is the variation of a specific gene that results in observable traits. For example, in bachelor's buttons blue is the dominant color. Seeds harvested from multi-colored stands that have been allowed to cross-pollinate will eventually produce plants with a majority of blue flowers.

<u>Recessive trait</u>, abbreviated "r", is variation of a specific gene that results in observable traits only if the dominant variation is not present. For example, wrinkled pea seeds only result when the dominant, smooth-seed trait is missing.

HARVEST: Successful production of seeds may require a growing season several weeks longer than the successful production of an individual vegetable or flower. Plan accordingly. For example, start plants indoors and design a strategy to allow enough time before frosts for the maturation of seeds.

<u>Viable seeds</u> are seeds that germinate and produce vigorous plants. Seeds should not be harvested before they have matured enough to be viable.

<u>Dehiscent</u> seed capsules are open and discharging seeds. Seeds must be harvested before this stage takes place and seeds are lost. Seed capsules in some varieties literally explode at the point of maturity. It is common to have only a few capsules out of hundreds mature at any one time.

PROCESS: Cleaning and separating seeds from chaff is not difficult or even necessary for small, home garden needs. Often, a little extra time taken during harvest to shake seeds out, one capsule at a time, results in completely clean seeds that need no processing.

<u>Thresh</u> is a term used by seed professionals to describe the process of separating seeds from chaff, the small, remaining pieces of pods or coverings.

<u>Flail</u> is the process of fracturing or crushing seed pods in order to free the seeds. This can take the form of everything from simply rubbing broccoli pods between hands to walking or even driving over bean vines.

<u>Winnow</u> is an ancient technique used to clean seeds. Seeds and chaff are poured through moving air which blows the lighter chaff aside, allowing the heavier seeds to be collected below.

<u>Cleaning Screens</u> with different-sized openings are used to separate seeds from chaff. The screen number denotes the number of openings that will cover a one inch line. First "scalp" by selecting a screen with openings just large enough to let seeds

drop through without the chaff then "sift" by using a screen that allows dirt and the small chaff to drop through without the seeds.

STORAGE: The successful storage of seeds demands cool, dark, and dry conditions. Make sure seeds have dried before putting them in plastic bags. Remember to label and date them. Note: plastic bags alone do not protect against moisture in moist locations like refrigerators or freezers. Allow jars that have been stored in a refrigerator or freezer to warm to room temperature before opening to prevent moist air from condensing on the inside walls of the jar.

Cool: At the National Seed Storage Laboratory in Ft. Collins, Colorado, some seeds are stored at 400° F. below zero. However, generally, storage conditions are adequate if seeds are kept below 50° F. Most importantly, always keep your seeds below 80°F, the temperature seeds begin to die off more quickly.

Dark: Absolute darkness is best. However, seed storage is adequate if direct sunlight or bright, artificial light is avoided.

Dry: Dryness is the most important factor in the long-term storage of seeds. State of the art seed banks design levels to be at or below 25% moisture. Most vegetable and flower seeds can be stored in drier climates without special protection, especially if packaged on dry days and put in glass or moisture proof plastic containers. Silica can also be used for prolonged storage in humid climates. Do not vacuum pack your seeds. They are living, breathing embryos.

CHAPTER III

BEGINNING SEED SAVER'S VEGETABLES

The vegetables in this chapter offer the beginning gardener the best chance for successful seed saving. These vegetables are annuals and produce seed the same season as planted. They are mostly self-pollinating (selfers), minimizing the need to be mindful of preventing cross-pollination.

BEAN

Phaseolus vulgaris

PLANT: Although, ideally, different varieties should be separated by 150 feet or another crop flowering at the same time, we rarely observe cross-pollination even when two varieties are grown next to each other.

FLOWER: Beans produce perfect, self-pollinating flowers. Cross pollination by insects is possible but rare as pollination occurs before the flower opens. Because the anthers are pushed up against the stigma, automatic pollination is assured when the anthers open.

SELECTION TRAITS: Most commercial breeders favor bush varieties which can be mechanically harvested and fibrous bean pods which hold up during harvest and shipment. Pole varieties are more suited to small, home gardens because they produce more beans in a smaller space. Because vines are off the ground beans are easier to pick and away from the settling cold air of unexpected frosts.   Plant growth: Pole type growth, D; Bush, r. Pod edibility: Little or no fiber, r; Stringless, r . Seed color: White seeded varieties are better for canning because seed color doesn't affect canning liquid, r; Colored, D. Pod, foliage and flower color: Purple, D.

HARVEST: Allow pods to dry brown before harvesting, about six weeks after eating stage. If frost threatens, pull entire plant, root first, and hang in cool, dry location until pods are brown.

PROCESS: Small amounts of pods can be opened by hand. Flail larger amounts. Remove large chaff by hand or fork. Winnow remaining particles.

LETTUCE

Lactuca sativa

PLANT: Separate varieties flowering at the same time by at least 20 feet to ensure purity.

FLOWER: Lettuce produces perfect, self-pollinating flowers. Each flower produces one seed. Flowers are grouped in little heads of 10-25 flowers all of which open at once for as little as 30 minutes. Anthers are fused together into a little cone that completely surrounds stigma and style. Style is pushed up through anther cone and is coated with its own pollen. Note: Mature head lettuce may need a slit (two or three inches deep) across the top to encourage flowering.

SELECTION TRAITS: Leaf color: red, D. Leaf color is controlled by at least two genes with a number of variations possible. Generally, hybrids produced by crossing red and green varieties result in red offspring. Leaf shape: no lobes, D; oak leaved, r. Seed stalk formation: bolt resistance, r; Seed color: white seeds, r; black seeds, D.

HARVEST: Some outside leaves can be harvested for eating without harming seed production. Allow seed heads to dry 2-3 weeks after flowering. Individual heads will ripen at different times making the harvest of large amounts of seed at one time nearly impossible. Wait until half the flowers on each plant has gone to seed. Cut entire top of plant and allow to dry upside down in an open paper bag.

PROCESS: Small amounts of seed can be shaken daily from individual flowering heads. Rub with hands to remove remaining seeds. If necessary, separate seeds from chaff with screens.

PEA

Pisum sativum

PLANT: Ideally, different varieties need to be separated 50 feet or with another crop flowering at the same time. However, in the cool regions of the Rocky Mountains, we rarely observe cross-pollination even when two varieties are grown next to each other.

FLOWER: Peas produce perfect, self-pollinating flowers. Cross-pollination by insects is possible but rare because pollination occurs before the flower opens. Because the stigma does open before pollen is ready, crosses theoretically could occur.

SELECTION TRAITS: Most commercial breeders prefer bush varieties with pods that ripen simultaneously in order to facilitate commercial harvesting. Tall varieties produce more peas in small, home gardens. Plant Growth: tall, D; bush, r. Seed Shape: Round seeds germinate better in cold weather, D; wrinkled seeds, r. Pod Edibility: lack of fibers on the inside of the pod, r. Pod shape: round, D; flat, r.

HARVEST: Allow pods to dry brown before harvesting, about four weeks after eating stage. If frost threatens, pull entire plant, root first, and hang in cool, dry location until pods are brown.

PROCESS: Small amounts of pods can be opened by hand. Flail larger amounts. Remove large chaff by hand or fork. Winnow remaining particles.

PEPPER

Capsicum annuum, bell peppers, wax, cayenne, jalapeños, chiltepin
Capsicum frutescens, malagueta, tabasco and Thai peppers
Capsicum chinense, the hottest peppers, naga, habanero, Datil, Scotch bonnet
PLANT: Peppers have perfect, self-pollinating flowers. Even so, some areas of the country, i.e. the Southwest, report some crossing. Ask in your area. You will get satisfactory results if different varieties are separated by another flowering crop. Space varieties at least 400 feet with other flowering crops for commercial quality.
FLOWER: Peppers produce perfect, mostly self-pollinating flowers. Solitary bees can increase crossing if a more desirable pollen is not available in the area.
SELECTION TRAITS: Flavor: Hot, D
HARVEST: Harvest mature, fully-ripe peppers for seed. (Most bell peppers turn red when fully mature.) If frost threatens before peppers mature, pull entire plant and hang in cool, dry location until fruits mature.
PROCESS: Allow pepper fruits to dry completely. Mature seeds will turn a beautiful golden color. Cut the bottom off the fruit or break it open. Carefully reach in to strip the seeds surrounding the central cone. If done carefully, the seeds will need no further cleaning. Note: In areas with late season rain or higher humidity, carefully cut vertical slits in each fruit to help dry the inside before fungus attacks the seeds. Warning: Use gloves and adequate respiration mask when processing hot peppers.

TOMATO

Solanum lycopersicum
PLANT: Separate varieties with short styles (most modern varieties) by at least 10 feet. Varieties with long styles (heirlooms and older varieties) need at least 100 feet to ensure purity. If solitary bees are prevalent, separate all varieties at least 100 feet and place another flowering crop between.
FLOWER: Tomatoes produce perfect, self-pollinating flowers. Anthers are fused together into a little cone that rarely opens until pollen has been shed and the stigma pollinated. (Older varieties with wild tomatoes or *S. pimpinellifolium* in their genetic ancestry may have stigmas that stick out beyond the cone containing the anthers. Varieties with this trait can be identified by looking closely at mature flowers to see the protruding stigma.)
SELECTION TRAITS: Tomato is the most popular vegetable in America and hundreds of the genes have been mapped. Those of immediate importance for home gardeners include: Plant size: Determinate varieties, r; bush varieties, r; dwarf varieties, r. Leaf Shape: Potato-type leaves, r. Disease resistance: Leaf mold resistance, r; fusarium wilt, race 1 and race 2, D; verticillium wilt, D; alternaria, D; tobacco mosaic, D; nematodes, D. Ripening: prevents green shoulders, r; prevents

ripening and is found in Longkeeper, r; produces parthenocarpic fruits which do not need to be pollinated. Tomatoes without seeds can be produced in weather too-cold for pollination to take place, r. Fruit color: Produced by the combination of flesh and skin colors:

red: pink flesh, r covered by a yellow skin, r
pink: pink flesh, r and colorless skin, r
crimson: bright, purplish-red flesh, r and yellow skin, r
purple: bright, purplish-red flesh, r and colorless skin, r;
yellow: yellowish flesh, r and yellow skin, r
white: yellowish flesh, r and colorless skin, r
orange: reddish-orange flesh, D and yellow skin, r

HARVEST: If possible, allow tomatoes to completely ripen before harvesting for seed production. Unripe fruits, saved from the first frost, will ripen slowly if kept in a cool, dry location. Seeds from green, unripe fruits can be viable if extracted after allowing the fruits to mature for several weeks.

PROCESS: Cut the tomato into halves at its equator, opening the vertical cavities that contain the seeds. Gently squeeze out from the cavities the jelly-like substance that contains the seeds. If done carefully, the tomato itself can still be eaten or saved for canning, sun-drying or dehydrating.

Place the jelly and seeds into a small jar or glass. (Add a little water if you are processing only one or two small tomatoes.) Loosely cover the container and place in a warm location, 60-75° F. for about three days. Stir once a day.

A layer of fungus will begin to appear on the top of the mixture after a couple of days. This fungus not only eats the gelatinous coat that surrounds each seed and prevents germination, it also produces antibiotics that help to control seed-borne diseases like bacterial spot, canker and speck.

After three days fill the seed container with warm water. Let the contents settle and begin pouring out the water along with pieces of tomato pulp and immature seeds floating on top.   Note: Viable seeds are heavier and settle to the bottom of the jar. Repeat this process until water being poured out is almost clear and clean seeds line the bottom of the container. Pour these clean seeds into a strainer that has holes smaller than the seeds. Let the excess water drip out and invert the strainer onto paper towel or piece of newspaper. Allow the seeds to dry completely (usually a day or two). Break up the clumps into individual seeds, label and store in a packet or plastic bag.

CHAPTER IV
INTERMEDIATE SEED SAVER'S VEGETABLES

This section addresses vegetables producing seed the same season they are planted but require separation to keep unwanted cross-pollination from taking place.

CORN
Zea mays

PLANT: Female corn flowers are pollinated predominately by the wind, rarely by insects. Pollen is light and can be carried great distances. For commercial quality, separate two varieties pollinating at the same time by at least 1 mile, or stagger planting dates at least 3-4 weeks. Reasonable results are obtained with separation of 1000 feet, especially if varieties are planted perpendicular to prevailing winds.

FLOWER: Corn is monecious, producing separate male and female flowers on each plant. Male flowers appear as tassels on the top of corn stalks and female flowers are pollinated via the silk emerging from each ear.

INBREEDING DEPRESSION: Corn is susceptible to intense inbreeding depression. If seed is saved from too few plants, subsequent plants may be short, mature late and produce few ears. The minimum number of plants necessary to maintain a healthy population is debated. Grow at least 200 plants and save the seeds from at least 100 of the best as a minimum. Professionals now prefer at least 500 plants as a minimum for seed bank accessions.

SELECTION TRAITS: Although corn genetics have been extensively studied, most meaningful traits are controlled by numerous genes and exact explanations are complicated. The following are general predictions: kernel sweetness: (su) sweet flavor (wrinkled seed), r, (sh2) shrunken, extreme sweetness (wrinkled seed), r, (se) supersweet, (delays starch formation), r
kernel color: black, D (results in black or blue); colored, D (over white); white, r.
kernel starch: flint, D; sweet corn, r.

HARVEST: Corn seed is usually ready to be harvested 4-6 weeks after eating stage. If growing season is not long enough, pick ears after husks turn brown. Pull back husks and complete drying in cool, dry location.

PROCESS: Process all but very large amounts of seed by gripping dried ears by hand and twisting with hand corn sheller. Kernels will fall into container. Any remaining silk and chaff can be winnowed.

CUCUMBER

Cucumis sativus (All cucumbers except Armenian cucumbers)
PLANT: Separate two different cucumber varieties by at least 1/2 mile to ensure purity. Experienced, home, seed savers can grow more than one variety at a time in a single garden by using hand pollinating techniques.
FLOWER: Cucumbers are mostly monoecious with separate male and female flowers on each plant. Female flowers can be identified by locating the ovary (a small looking cucumber) at the base of the flower. Cucumber vines will produce the greatest amount of female flowers when day length shortens to approximately 11 hours per day. Fruits will be aborted during dry spells and very hot weather.
INBREEDING DEPRESSION: Although inbreeding depression is not usually noticeable in cucumbers, seeds should be saved from at least 6 cucumbers on 6 different plants.
HARVEST: Cucumbers raised for seed cannot be eaten. They should be left to ripen at least 5 weeks after eating stage until they have turned a golden color. First, light frost of the season will blacken vines and make cucumbers easier to find. Undamaged fruits can be stored in cool, dry place for several weeks to finish ripening.
PROCESS: Slice fruit lengthwise and scrape seeds out with a spoon. Allow seeds and jelly-like liquid to sit in jar at room temperature for 3 or 4 days. Fungus will start to form on top. Stir daily. Jelly will dissolve and good seeds will sink to bottom while remaining debris and immature seeds can be rinsed away. Spread seeds on a paper towel or screen until dry. (See instructions for tomato on page 13-14.)

MUSKMELON

Cucumis melo (Divided below into seven separate groups because of similar features. All *C. melos* varieties in all groups will cross with each other. They will not cross with watermelons which are *Citrullus vulgaris*.
Indorus: honeydew, crenshaw, casaba
Conomon: Asian, pickling melons
Dundaim: pocket melon
Cantalupensis: true cantelopes (without netted skin)
Flexuosus: Armenian cucumbers
Reticulatus: Persian melons, muskmelons with netted skin and orange flesh
Chito: orange melon, garden lemon melon
PLANT: Separate two different muskmelons by at least 1/2 mile to ensure purity. Experienced, home, seed savers grow more than one variety at a time in a single garden by using hand pollinating techniques. Muskmelon flowers are small and relatively difficult to hand pollinate.
FLOWER: Muskmelons are mostly monoecious with separate male and female flowers on each plant. (Some female flowers have stamens.) Female flowers can be identified by locating the ovary (a small looking melon) at the base of the flower.

The early flowers are the most likely to be successfully pollinated and eventually produce seeds.

INBREEDING DEPRESSION: Not usually a problem with muskmelons.

HARVEST: Muskmelon seed is mature and can be harvested from ripe and ready to eat muskmelons.

PROCESS: Simply rinse seeds clean, dry with towel and spread on board or cookie sheet to complete drying.

RADISH
Raphanus sativus

PLANT: Separate different varieties being grown for seed at the same time by at least 1/2 mile to ensure purity. Satisfactory results for home gardeners require no more that 250 feet of separation. As radishes cannot self-pollinate, pollen must be carried by insects from plant to plant. Seed to seed: Mulch in the fall to insure winter survival. The following spring, thin to 9" spacing, leaving those roots that showed no sign of bolting. Root to seed: Harvest roots in fall. Select desirable roots and trim tops to within an inch of the roots leaving small, new leaves. Store at 40° F. in humid location. Replant in early spring at 9" intervals and cover with 1" of soil. Note: Garden varieties of radish will cross with wild varieties.

FLOWER: Radishes produce annual flowers which require pollination by insects, primarily bees.

HARVEST: Harvest 3' tall stalks when pods have dried brown. Pull entire plant and hang in cool, dry place if all pods are not dried at the end of the growing season.

PROCESS: Open pods by hand for small amounts of seed. Pods that do not open when rubbed between hands can be pounded with hammer or mallet. Winnow to remove remaining chaff.

SPINACH
Spinacia oleracae

PLANT: It is probably best to grow seeds for only one variety of spinach at a time. Commercial seed crops are separated 5 miles or more. Plant early in the spring to allow enough time for seed production which can take 4-6 weeks more than the time required to reach eating stage. Remove plants which bolt first, and thin remaining plants to 8" for seed production. Leave one male plant for each two females to ensure pollination.

FLOWER: Spinach is "dioecious" with male and female flowers on separate plants. Flowers are wind pollinated by spinach's dust-like, powdery pollen which can be carried for miles.

SELECTION TRAITS: Seed shape: prickly, smooth. Leaf texture: flat, wrinkled.

HARVEST: Some outside leaves can be harvested for eating without harming seed

production. If possible, wait until all plants have dried brown. Pull entire plant and hang in cool, dry place if necessary at the end of the growing season.
PROCESS: Strip seeds in upward motion and let them fall into container. Chaff can be winnowed. Use gloves for prickly-seeded types.

SQUASH / PUMPKIN

Cucurbita maxima varieties with large, hairy leaves, long vines and soft, hairy stems and include: banana squashes, buttercups, hubbards and marrows
Cucurbita argyrosperma (mixta) varieties with large, hairy leaves, long vines and hard, hairy stems and include: cushaws
Cucurbita moschata varieties similar to *C. mixta* with flaring stems at the fruit and large, green sepals surrounding the flowers and include: butternuts
Cucurbita pepo varieties with prickly stems and leaves with a hard, five-angled stem and include: acorn squashes, cocozelles, pumpkins, crooknecks, scallops, spaghetti squashes and zucchinis
PLANT: Squashes from different species (see above) can be grown next to each other. Separate different squash varieties in the same species by at least 1/2 mile to ensure purity. (Some crossing between *C. argyrosperma* and *C. moschata* has been reported. We know of none from our own experience and have concluded that this is a rare event.) Ask in your area. Experienced, home, seed savers grow more than one variety in a single garden by using hand pollinating techniques. Squash flowers are large and relatively easy to hand pollinate with a little paint brush. Tape them shut before and after hand pollinating to prevent insect pollination.
FLOWER: Squashes are monoecious with male flowers and female flowers on each plant. Female flowers can be identified by locating the ovary (a small looking squash) at the base of the flower. (Some female flowers have stamens.)
INBREEDING DEPRESSION: Not usually noticed in squash and pumpkins.
HARVEST: Squash must be fully mature before harvested for seed production. This means that summer squashes must be left on the vine until outer shell hardens. Allow to cure 3-4 additional weeks after harvest to encourage further seed ripening.
PROCESS: Chop open hard-shelled fruits and scoop out seeds. Rinse clean in wire strainer with warm, running water. Dry with towel and spread on board or cookie sheet to complete drying.

CHAPTER V

ADVANCED SEED SAVER'S VEGETABLES

Advanced gardener's vegetables normally require more than one year for seed production and mandate separation to prevent cross-pollination.

BEET / SWISS CHARD

Beta vulgaris
PLANT: Grow seed for only one variety of beet or Swiss chard at any one time. Seed to seed: Mulch first year crop in the fall to ensure winter survival. The following spring, thin to 18" spacing. Root to seed: Harvest roots in fall. Select desirable roots and trim tops 1-2" above root. Store at 40° F. in humid location. Replant in early spring at 18" intervals with tops just showing above the soil.
FLOWER: Beets and Swiss chard produce perfect flowers. Pollen is light and can be carried for miles by the wind.
INBREEDING DEPRESSION: Save seed from at least 6 different beets to ensure genetic diversity and vigor.
SELECTION TRAITS: Root color: red, red with white stripes, pink, gold, and yellow. Root shape: round, cylindrical.
HARVEST: Cut 4' tall tops just above the root when majority flowering clusters have turned brown. Tops can be stored in cool, dry locations for 2-3 weeks to encourage further seed ripening.
PROCESS: Small quantities of seed can be stripped by hand as seed matures. Large numbers of tops can be put into a cloth bag and stomped or pounded. Chaff can be winnowed.

BROCCOLI / BRUSSELS SPROUT / CAULIFLOWER CABBAGE / KALE

Brassica napus pabularia, Siberian kale, red Russian kale
Brassica oleracea, broccoli, Brussels sprout, cauliflower, cabbage, kale
PLANT: Vegetables and varieties listed above within each species will cross with

one another. Separate different varieties at least 1000 feet for satisfactory results or at least 1 mile for purity. Caging with introduced pollinators or alternate day caging is also recommended in small gardens. Plants to be left for seed production should be mulched in the fall or carefully dug, trimmed and stored for the winter in humid area with temperatures between 35-40° F. Flowering plants can reach 4' in height and need at least 2' spacing for good seed production.

FLOWER: With the exception of early-season broccolis and cauliflowers, most *B. oleracea* and *nappus* varieties require vernalization (cold, winter-like temperatures for several weeks) before flowering occurs. Flowers are perfect, most of which cannot be self-pollinated. Necessary cross-pollination is performed by bees. The stigma becomes receptive before the flower opens, and pollen is shed hours after the flower opens.

INBREEDING DEPRESSION: Plant at least 6 different plants to protect vigor and ensure a reasonable amount of genetic diversity.

SELECTION TRAITS: Plant characteristics: tall, D; side buds, D. Plant color: purple, green, magenta. Leaf shape: wide, entire, smooth, hairy.

HARVEST: Broccoli, cauliflower, cabbage and kohlrabi heads grown for seed should not be trimmed for consumption. Brussels sprouts, collards and kale can be lightly trimmed for eating without affecting quality seed production. If small amounts of seeds are wanted, allow individual pods to dry to a light brown color before picking and opening by hand. Lower pods dry first followed by those progressively higher on the plant. For larger amounts of seeds pull entire plant after a majority of pods have dried. Green pods rarely produce viable seeds even if allowed to dry after the plant is pulled.

PROCESS: Smash unopened pods in cloth bag with mallet or by walking on them. Chaff can be winnowed.

CARROT
Daucus carota

PLANT: Separate different varieties at least 1/2 mile to ensure purity. (Queen Anne's Lace or wild carrot will cross with garden carrot.) Alternate day caging or caging with introduced pollinators allows two or more varieties to be grown for seed in small gardens. Seed to seed: Plant seeds in mid-summer. Finger-sized carrots are more winter hardy than full-grown carrots. Mulch in late-fall to ensure winter survival. Thin to 30" spacing in the spring. Root to seed: Harvest eating-sized roots in fall for replanting in fall or early spring. Mulch if planted in fall. Clip tops to 1-2" and store at 35-40° F. in humid location or layered in sawdust or sand. Replant roots with desirable characteristics 30" apart with soil just covering shoulders. **FLOWER:** Carrots produce perfect flowers that are cross-pollinated by a number of insects. Flowers are arranged in round, flat groups called umbels. Carrots require vernalization (cold, winter-like temperatures for several weeks) before flowering occurs.

INBREEDING DEPRESSION: Carrots can exhibit severe inbreeding depression.

Save and mix seed from as many different carrots as possible.
SELECTION TRAITS: Root color: white, D; black, orange, purple, red, yellow, r. Root shape: tapered, triangular, round, stubby.
HARVEST: For small amounts, hand pick each umbel as it dries brown. Large amounts of seed can be harvested by cutting entire flowering top as umbels begin to dry. Allow to mature in cool, dry location for an additional 2-3 weeks.
PROCESS: Clean small amounts by rubbing between hands. Larger amounts can be beaten from stalks and umbels. Screen and winnow to clean. Carrot seed is naturally hairy or "bearded". Debearding in the cleaning process does not affect germination.

ESCAROLE / FRISSEE
Chichorium endivia
PLANT: Separate different varieties at least 1/2 mile to ensure purity. Caging with introduced pollinators allows two or more varieties to be grown for seed in small gardens. Cages must be left on for entire flowering season. Although *C. endivia* is a biennial, cold, short days during the first spring will sometimes cause bolting. See: radicchio/Belgian endive.
FLOWER: Perfect, mostly-self-pollinating flowers. Pollen from *C. endivia* will pollinate *C. intybus* (radicchio), however *C. endivia* will not be pollinated by *C. intybus*.
HARVEST: A few outside leaves can be harvested for eating without harming seed production. Allow plants to dry completely after most of the flowers have set pods. Pry open pods to release dry, hard seeds.
PROCESS: Small amounts of seed can be left in pods and replanted. Some thinning will be required. Crush large amounts of pods in cloth bag with wooden mallet. Screen and winnow to remove debris.

ONION
Varieties within each onion species will cross with each other. Crosses between species although not common, are possible.
Allium schoenoprasum: Common chives
Allium tuberosum: Garlic chives
Allium fistulosum: Japanese bunching onions (Occasional crossing between *A. fistulosum* and *A. cepa* has been observed.)
Allium cepa comprised of three groups: Aggregatum includes shallots, multiplier onions and potato onions; Cepa our biennial, common storage and slicing onions; Proliferum includes the Egyptian or walking onions.
PLANT: Separate from other flowering *Alliums* of the same species at least 1000 feet for satisfactory results or at least 1 mile for purity. Caging with introduced pol-

linators or alternate day caging is also recommended in small gardens. Seed to seed:
Plant seeds in late-spring or early-summer. Immature onions are more winter hardy
than larger, full-grown bulbs. Mulch in late-fall to ensure winter survival. Thin to
12" spacing in the spring. Root to seed: Harvest in the fall and select the largest
bulbs which produce more seed. Clip tops to 6" and store at 35-40° F. in dry, airy
location. Replant in early spring with 12" spacing. Cover bulbs with 1/2" soil.

FLOWER: The *Alliums* produce perfect flowers, most of which are cross-pollinated because stigmas in each flower become receptive only after pollen in that flower
is shed. Flowers in an individual umbel open and shed pollen at different times so
crosses can and do occur on the same plant. Cross-pollination is performed mostly
by bees. Many onions require vernalization (cold, winter-like temperatures for
several weeks) before flowering occurs. Store for at least two weeks in a refrigerator.
INBREEDING DEPRESSION: Onions display a fair amount of inbreeding depression after two or three generations of self-pollination. Save and mix the seeds
from at least two different plants.
SELECTION TRAITS: Bulb color: white, D; buff, red, yellow, r.
HARVEST: Clip umbels as soon as majority of flowers have dried. Seeds will start
dropping from some flowers at this time so check often. Allow to dry in cool, dry
location for up to 2-3 weeks.
PROCESS: Fully dried flowers will drop clean seeds naturally. For small amounts,
rub remaining flowers to free seeds. For larger amounts, rub heads over screens.
Winnow to remove remaining debris.

RADICCHIO / BELGIAN ENDIVE
WITLOOF CHICORY
Cichorium intybus
PLANT: Isolate different varieties by 1/2 mile to ensure purity. Pollen from esca-
role and frisee, *C. endivia*, will contaminate *C. intybus* and must also be isolated.
Wild chicory will cross and should be eliminated. Seed to seed: Mulch in late-fall to
insure winter survival. Thin to 18" spacing in the spring. Root to seed: Harvest in
the fall and select the best roots. Clip tops to 2" and store at 35-40° F. in humid location for up to 3 months. Replant in early spring with 18" spacing.
FLOWER: Although chicory flowers are perfect, they do not self-pollinate. Insects
perform cross-pollination.
HARVEST: A few outside leaves can be harvested for eating without harming seed
production. Allow plants to dry completely after most of the flowers have set pods.
Pry open pods to release dry, hard seeds.
PROCESS: Radicchio seed is difficult to remove from the pods. The entire pod can
be planted without removing the seeds, but some of the numerous seedlings emerging in each location will need to be thinned. Crush large amounts of pods in cloth
bag with wooden mallet. Screen and winnow to remove debris.

TURNIP / CHINESE CABBAGE

Brassica campestris (formerly *B. rapa*) (*B. campestris* varieties, divided below into five separate groups because of similar features, will cross with each other.)

Rapifera: root turnips

Ruvo: flower-stalk turnips including Italian turnips, rapa and broccoli raab

Chinensis: nonheading varieties of Chinese mustard including pak choi and celery mustard

Pekinensis: heading varieties of Chinese cabbage

Perviridis: spinach mustards

PLANT: Separate *B. campestris* varieties at least 1000 feet for satisfactory results or at least 1/2 mile for purity. Caging with introduced pollinators or alternate day caging is also recommended in small gardens. Seed to seed: Plants left for seed production should be mulched in the fall. Flowering plants can grow 3' tall and need at least 2' spacing for good seed production. Root to seed: Carefully dig roots in the fall, trim tops to 2" and store for the winter in humid location (layered in sand or sawdust) with temperatures 35-40° F. Replant best roots in early spring with 2' spacing.

FLOWER: The *B. campestris* species produces perfect flowers, most of which cannot be self-pollinated. Cross-pollination is performed mostly by bees. The stigma becomes receptive before the flower opens. Pollen is shed hours after the flower opens. *B. campestris* varieties require vernalization (cold, winter-like temperatures for several weeks) before flowering occurs. Store for at least four weeks in a refrigerator.

INBREEDING DEPRESSION: Plant at least 6 different plants to ensure a reasonable amount of genetic diversity.

HARVEST: Turnips grown for seed should not be trimmed for eating. Chinese cabbage can be lightly trimmed for eating without affecting quality seed production. If small amounts of seeds are wanted, allow individual pods to dry to a light brown color before picking and opening by hand. Lower pods dry first followed by those progressively higher on the plant. For larger amounts of seeds pull entire plant after a majority of pods have dried. Green pods rarely produce viable seeds even if allowed to dry after the plant is pulled.

PROCESS: Smash unopened pods in a cloth bag with mallet or by walking on them. Chaff can be winnowed.

CHAPTER VI

WILDFLOWER SEED COLLECTING

Wildflower seed collecting is not especially mysterious or difficult. Probing, poking, shaking, and crushing unfamiliar dried pods and capsules can lead to new challenges and satisfying successes. With few exceptions, all flowers eventually produce seeds that can be harvested. Amateur seed collectors need only look to find them.

ECOLOGICALLY SENSITIVE SEED COLLECTING:

Collect the seeds from no more than one-third of the plants in a population. If there are only a few plants in a given area, don't take more than one-third of the seeds from any one plant. Never disturb single displays or plants identified as sensitive or endangered.

Note that it is legal for individuals to collect seeds on public land, provided they not rare or endangered. If you wish to collect on private property, always get the permission of the landowner. Emphasize that you are interested only in seeds.

If you are unsure of a plant's status, check with the nearest native plant society, or the nearest office of the Nature Conservancy—both keep databases on local flora.

IDENTIFICATION:

Unfortunately for amateur seed collectors, most flower guides describe and picture plants during their flowering stage, long before seeds are mature enough to be collected. If you stumble across a plant that interests you, but it has already gone to seed, don't leave it behind just because you can't identify it.

Try searching the immediate area for different members of the same species that may be still flowering—fortunately, this is a common occurrence. In some cases, seeds that are dried and ready to be collected are right next to flower buds just beginning to open.

In the mountains, you'll find wildflower seeds dried and ready to be collected at lower elevations, while the same plant is in full bloom farther up the mountain. A seed collector can, in effect, move back in time by climbing to a higher elevation— and thereby solve the mystery of the plant's identity.

Another trick used by seed collectors is to look in and around a patch of plants to find the previous year's dried stalks and seedpods. Even if the seeds have long since disappeared, important clues can be discovered as to the shape and size of the coming flowers.

If you are still unable to identify a plant, don't worry. You will be able to later when you raise it at home and observe all of its growth stages at your leisure.

Please note that the information necessary for the identification of wildflowers at a *species* level is beyond the scope of this booklet. A good field guide will be helpful, or perhaps you can show your wildflower to someone knowledgeable. In the end, don't fret too much about complete species identification. The point is to get to know and learn to grow these plants yourself.

TAGGING:

If you find plants in the flowering stage that you want to collect seed from later, mark each one at the base with a colorful ribbon or string so you can relocate them. Our experience is that without such tags, plants can be difficult to identify even a short time after their blossoms have dried or dropped.

TIMING:

Timing is important for successful wildflower collecting. Generally speaking, you must harvest when the seeds are ripe, or dry. In extreme situations, bountiful quantities of seeds found one day completely disappear the next.

Observe the sequence in which wildflowers bloom each year. The "start date" may change because spring comes early or late. Once the sequence has begun, the different species will bloom in the same order, year after year, allowing you to predict the best seed-collecting time. For example, if Lupine is usually ready for seed collection a week after Arrowleaf Balsamroot, and Arrowleaf Balsamroot is two weeks later than usual, Lupine will also be ready two weeks later than usual.

KEEPING RECORDS:

Always keep detailed records about each seed-collecting trip and each seed sample. If possible, carry small envelopes or bags, an indelible-ink pen, and a notebook. Put each seed sample in its own bag and label it with the following information: date, location, elevation, surrounding vegetation, soil, estimated total of plants in the area, and other relevant comments. Note the same information, in more detail if you wish, in your field notebook along with a story about the day.

COLLECTING SEEDS:

Collect small quantities of seed carefully and threshing and cleaning will not be necessary. A little extra time taken when harvesting will save tremendous amounts of time later. Whenever possible, bend fully mature stalks into open seed-collecting bags and shake lightly. Nearly pure seed can be collected in this manner.

KEY

(A) = annual, (B) = biennial, (P) = perennial

CHAPTER VII

WILDFLOWERS

ARNICA

Arnica cordifolia (P)
The most medicinal Arnica found in the Western U.S. An excellent ground cover when grown thickly in par-tially shaded locations.
FLOWER: Large, yellow, daisy-like flower framed by two opposite, soft, heart-shaped leaves. Plant grows 8" to 12" tall. Blooms: second year, June to July.
SEED: When fully mature, small, dandelion-like parachutes collectively puff into a dome shape. Seed will be viable if harvested early, before the yellow flower petals have completely dried. Slightest wind or rain will scatter mature seeds.
COLLECTION: Pick each mature seed dome by hand to avoid later cleaning. Or pick the yellow flowers themselves and allow them to dry in a paper bag, where they will magically turn into seed heads.
PROCESSING: Separation of the seeds from petals and small debris is difficult if not impossible without expensive equipment.

ARROWLEAF BALSAMROOT

Balsamorhiza sagittata (P)
FLOWER: Yellow, 2" to 3" flowers are framed by large, light-green leaves that are shaped like arrowheads. Plant grows to 2 1/2' tall. Blooms: second or third year, May to July.
SEED: Black, sunflower-like, 1/4" long. When mature, seeds hold up fairly well for up to 10 days, if not eaten by horses.
COLLECTION: Shake fully-mature heads into an open bag to minimize the need for cleaning. Large amounts are best collected by pulling entire seed heads after yellow petals have dropped. Wear gloves to protect hands from damage due to the spiny, dry nature of the seed heads.
PROCESSING: Allow heads to completely dry before lightly bouncing on a #6 or #8 cleaning screen. Winnowing will remove some of the remaining debris.

ASTER

Aster tanacetifolia (A)
FLOWER: Showy, bright, daisylike purple flowers with yellow centers. Plant grows to 1 1/2' tall. Blooms: July to October.
SEED: Small, dandelionlike parachutes puff into a fragile domes. Slightest wind or rain will scatter mature seeds.
COLLECTION: Pick each mature seed dome by hand to avoid later cleaning. The purple flowers can be picked and allowed to dry in a paper bag, where they will magically turn into seed heads.
PROCESSING: The separation of seeds from petals and small debris is difficult if not impossible without expensive equipment.

BABY'S-BREATH

Gypsophila paniculata (P)
FLOWER: Hundreds of very small, lacy white flowers cover sage-green shrubs. A single plant can measure 3' by 3'. Blooms: second year, July to September.
Gypsophila muralis (A)
FLOWER: White flowers are larger than *G. paniculata* on a smaller (2') plant. Blooms: June to September.
SEED: To the unaided eye, seeds look similar to cabbage seeds—black, hard, round, 1/16" in diameter.
COLLECTION: Wait until the majority of seedpods turn brown and seed is beginning to fall. Collect early in the day, as morning dew helps keep mature seeds from falling. Carefully shake the bush over an open bag.
PROCESSING: Rub unopened pods on a #16 screen. Winnow remaining debris.

BACHELOR'S BUTTON

Centaurea cyanus (A) Cornflower.
FLOWER: Brilliant, multi-colored, 1" to 2" puffs top slender stems with gray-green foliage. Blue is dominant color over pink, and pink over white. Plant grows 1' to 2' tall. Blooms: August to September.
SEED: Yellow-and-gray cylinders, 1/8" long, with blond, 1/8" hairs (pappus) sticking straight out at one end. Once mature, seed heads shatter easily.
COLLECTION: Carefully shake mature heads into an open bag to avoid further cleaning. Nearly-mature heads can be picked whole and allowed to finish drying in a paper bag.
PROCESSING: Shake through a #12 screen and winnow remaining debris.

BEAR GRASS

Xerophyllum tenax (P)
FLOWER: Creamy-white plumes. Plant grows 2' to 4' tall. Blooms: second or third year, July to August.

SEED: Look like tan-colored canoes, 1/8" long. Open capsules are little cups that hold mature seeds for at least two or three weeks (in the absence of wind or rain). **COLLECTION:** Carefully shake mature heads into an open bag to avoid further cleaning. Large amounts of seed can be collected in this manner. **PROCESSING:** Shake through a #12 screen and winnow remaining debris.

BLACK-EYED SUSAN

Rudbeckia hirta (P)
FLOWER: Daisylike blossoms with deep-yellow petals and dark-burgundy cones. Plant grows 2' to 3' tall. Blooms: July to September.
SEED: Black, shaped like a cucumber, 1/16" long. Thousands of seeds stand on end to form the black cone in the middle of a sunflowerlike blossom. Once mature (after yellow petals drop), seed heads shatter easily.
COLLECTION: Pick small amounts of pure seed from middle of cone with thumb and index finger. Collect large amounts by pulling entire heads.
PROCESSING: Shake through a #20 screen. Winnow remaining large debris.

CAMAS

Camassia quamash (P)
FLOWER: Brilliant, sky-blue camas blossoms annually transform our spring meadows into dazzling pools of color. Plant grows to 2 1/2' tall. Blooms: second year, May to June.
SEED: Black, pear-shaped, 1/8" long. Once open, the cuplike capsules hold seeds for up to two weeks. Seed is easily spilled if disturbed by wind or rain.
COLLECTION: Carefully shake mature heads into an open bag to avoid further cleaning. To collect large amounts of seed, snap off partially-opened capsules and put in a plastic bag.
PROCESSING: Allow capsules to dry fully; shake to remove remaining seeds, and winnow to remove small debris.

COLUMBINE

Aquilegia caerulea (P)
Colorado's state flower. Aptly named— "caerulea" means "blue."
FLOWER: Large, blue-and-white, 2" to 3" blossoms provide a spectacular show of color. Plant grows 2' to 3' tall. Blooms: second year, June to August.
Aquilegia vulgaris (P)
FLOWER: Delicate violet-pink-and-white blossoms. Dwarf plant, 8" to 16" tall. Blooms: second year, June to August.
Aquilegia formosa (P)
FLOWER: This small red flower with yellow, inner petals is a native of the Mountain West. Especially sweet and fragrant. Plant grows 1' to 2' tall. Blooms: second year, June to August.

SEED: Black, shiny, raisin-shaped, 1/16" long. Once open, the cuplike capsules hold seeds for up to three weeks. Seed is easily spilled if disturbed by wind or rain.
COLLECTION: Carefully shake mature heads into an open bag to avoid further cleaning. To collect large amounts of seed, snap off partially-opened capsules and put in a plastic bag.
PROCESSING: Allow capsules to completely dry on cookie sheets with sides. Shake to remove remaining seeds, and winnow to remove small debris.

COSMOS

Cosmos bipinnatus (A)
FLOWER: Numerous large pink blossoms and delicate, feathery, light-green foliage. Plant grows 3' to 5' tall. Darker colors are dominant. Blooms: July to first frost.
SEED: Black, pine-needle-shaped, 3/8" long. Seed heads shatter easily and seeds are lost soon after flower petals dry.
COLLECTION: Pick whole seed head just before seeds scatter and allow to finish drying.
PROCESSING: Shake dried seed heads to loosen remaining seeds.

DAISY, ASPEN

Erigeron speciosus (P)
FLOWER: Dainty, lilac-rayed, yellow-centered daisy populates open spaces in aspen country. 1' to 2' tall stems, each with a dozen or so 1" flowers. Blooms: July to August.
SEED: Blond, sunflowerlike, 1/16" long. Some have short, white hairs ("pappus"). Seed heads shatter easily and seeds are lost soon after flower petals dry.
COLLECTION: Carefully shake mature heads into an open bag to avoid further cleaning.
PROCESSING: Shake through a #20 screen. Winnow remaining large debris.

DAISY (OXEYE, SHASTA)

Chrysanthemum leucanthemum (P)
The classic, romantic, storybook daisy!
FLOWER: White, 1" petals surround bright-yellow buttons. Plant grows 1' to 3' tall. Blooms: second year, July to August.
Chrysanthemum maximum (P)
FLOWER: Similar to oxeye but with larger, 4" blossoms. Blooms: second year, July to August.
SEED: White-striped, cucumber-shaped . Oxeye daisy seeds are over 1/16" long; Shasta daisy seeds are 1/8" long. Seed heads shatter easily and seeds are lost soon after flower petals dry.
COLLECTION: Carefully shake mature heads into an open bag to avoid further cleaning.

PROCESSING: Shake through a #20 screen. Winnow remaining large debris.

DELPHINIUM
Delphinium occidentale (P)
FLOWER: Blue, 3/4" flowers, each with a tempting, hummingbird nectar tube.
Plant grows 3' to 6' tall. Blooms: July to August.
SEED: Black, wrinkled, raisin-shaped, 1/8" long. Once open, cuplike capsules hold
seeds for up to three weeks. Seed is easily spilled if disturbed by wind or rain.
COLLECTION: Carefully shake mature heads into an open bag to avoid further
cleaning. To collect large amounts, snap off opening capsules and put in a plastic
bag.
PROCESSING: Allow capsules to completely dry on cookie sheets with sides.
Shake to remove remaining seeds.

ELEPHANT-HEAD
Pedicularis groenlandica (P)
FLOWER: Numerous, satin-pink flowers, each miraculously resembling an
elephant's head (complete with "trunk" and "ears") encircle a 12" to 18" spike.
Blooms: second or third year, May to July.
SEED: Blond, raisin-shaped, 1/8" long. Once open, cuplike capsules hold seeds for
several weeks. Seed is easily spilled if disturbed by wind or rain.
COLLECTION: Carefully shake mature capsules into an open bag to avoid further
cleaning. To collect large amounts, snap off hard, brown capsules and put in a bag.
PROCESSING: Allow capsules to completely dry on cookie sheets with sides.
Shake to remove remaining seeds.

FIREWEED
Epilobium angustifolium (P)
FLOWER: Stunning pink blossoms (edible!). Plant grows 2' to 6' tall. Blooms:
June to September.
SEED: Blond specks, under 1/16" long, at the end of a cottony, well-developed
parachute.
COLLECTION: Gather the long, tubelike seedpods ("siliques") when dry enough
to shatter. Mature siliques can be found on the bottom of the panicle early in the
summer and higher as the season progresses.
PROCESSING: Debearding (separating from cottony parachute) is almost impos-
sible without special equipment. Unclean seed will germinate, however.

FLAX
Linum perenne subspecies *lewisii* (P)
FLOWER: Delicate blue blossoms with five silky petals on a lacy plant. Plant
grows 1' to 2' tall. Blooms: May to September.

Linum grandiflorum 'Rubrum' (A)
FLOWER: Breathtaking burgundy-red blossoms. Plant grows 2' tall. Blooms: July to September.
SEED: Shiny, black, oblong-shaped, 1/8" long. Once mature, each capsule holds about 10 seeds for a couple weeks.
COLLECTION: With gloves, pull capsules off plant; allow to finish drying and thresh with wooden mallet.
PROCESSING: Winnow to remove most debris.

GENTIAN, MOUNTAIN
Gentiana affinis (P)
FLOWER: Alpinists around the world know gentian's beautiful, little, blue, funnel-shaped flower. Plant grows 6" tall. Blooms: second year, July to September.
SEED: Blond, oval flakes, 1/16" long. Papery, funnel-shaped capsule holds seeds for several weeks after opening.
COLLECTION: Carefully shake clean seeds out of capsule. Collect large quantities by picking entire capsules, drying on cookie sheets, and shaking out remaining seeds.
PROCESSING: Lightly shake through a #30 screen.

GERANIUM, WILD
Geranium viscosissimum (P)
FLOWER: Delicate, pale-pink petals with deep-pink veins. Plant grows 1' to 3' tall. Blooms: second or third year, May to August.
SEED: Dull, black, blunt-ended, barrel-shaped, 1/8" long. The instant the seeds are fully mature, they are catapulted into space.
COLLECTION: Pick entire flower top as soon as or just before the petals drop. Flowers will finish maturing and seeds will be formed (and captured) if left to dry in partially covered, cool, dry location.
PROCESSING: Winnow to remove remaining debris.

GILIA, SCARLET
Gilia aggregata (also known as *Ipomopsis aggregata*) (B)
FLOWER: Dazzling red trumpets on thin spikes sound the beginning of summer. Plant grows 1' to 3' tall. Blooms: June to August.
SEED: Tan, angular, oblong-shaped, 1/16" to 1/8" long. As soon as mature, the cuplike capsules open and seed scatters. Few capsules on a single plant are ready for harvest at any one time.
COLLECTION: Carefully shake slightly opened capsules into an open bag.
PROCESSING: Rub lightly with hands to free remaining seeds.

INDIAN BLANKET
Gaillardia pulchella (A)

FLOWER: Brilliant-red daisies with flashy-yellow tips. Plant grows 18" to 24" tall. Blooms: July to September.
Gaillardia aristata (P)
FLOWER: Blooms: second year, June to August.
SEED: Tan, pointed, bristle-covered, 1/16" to 1/8" long, with 1/16" to 1/8" long white hairs ("pappus") opposite the point. Seed heads shatter easily and seeds are lost soon after flower petals dry.
COLLECTION: Carefully pick mature seed heads and allow to dry until clean seed falls out.
PROCESSING: Blow lightly to remove some of the remaining debris.

INDIAN PAINTBRUSH
Castilleja spp. (P)
FLOWER: Spectacular red-to-orange "paint-dipped" colors on erect stems. Plant grows to 2' tall. Blooms: second or third year, June to August.
Castilleja angustifolia (P)
FLOWER: Pale-pink bracts.
SEED: Blond, raisin-shaped, 1/16" long. Once open, the cuplike capsules hold seeds for several weeks. Seed is easily spilled if disturbed by wind or rain.
COLLECTION: Carefully shake mature capsules into an open bag to avoid further cleaning. To collect large amounts, snap off hard, brown capsules and put in a bag.
PROCESSING: Finish drying capsules on cookie sheet with sides. Shake to remove remaining seeds.

IRIS, ROCKY MOUNTAIN
Iris missouriensis (P)
FLOWER: Delicately sculpted blue-purple blossoms on long, slender stems. Plant grows 2' to 3' tall. Blooms: second or third year, May to July.
SEED: Burgundy, pear-shaped, over 1/8" long. Elongated capsules will actually hold seeds through the winter if not jostled by high winds. Insect damage can be a problem, however.
COLLECTION: Carefully massage mature capsules over an open bag to loosen seeds and avoid further cleaning. To collect large amounts, snap off the entire 2" to 3" tan capsules.
PROCESSING: Allow to dry completely and shake capsules or roll with your fingers to remove remaining seeds. Winnow to remove small debris.

LILY, SEGO
Calochortus eurycarpus (P)
One of nature's most exotic little flowers!
FLOWER: Silky white petals with touches of deep-purple, delicately perch on thin, nodding, green stalks. Seldom more than 12" tall. Blooms: third or fourth year, June

to August.
SEED: Blond, canoe-shaped, 1/8" long. Once open, the cuplike capsules hold seeds for several weeks. Seed is easily spilled if disturbed by wind or rain.
COLLECTION: Carefully shake into an open bag to avoid further cleaning. To collect large amounts of seed, snap off the entire, triangle-shaped capsules as they begin to open.
PROCESSING: Allow capsules to completely dry on cookie sheets with sides. Shake to remove remaining seeds.

LUPINE
Lupinus argenteus (P) Loose-flowered lupine.
FLOWER: Range of colors including white, yellow, and purple, sometimes on the same spike. Plant grows 12-24" tall. Blooms: second year, June to August.
L. sericeus (P) Silky lupine.
FLOWER: Beautiful blue, sweet-pea-like flowers crowd erect spikes. Plant grows 12-24" tall. Blooms: second year, June to August.
SEED: Flat, hard, slightly-wrinkled pea-shaped, over 1/8" in diameter, in a range of earthy tones. As soon as they begin to dry, the little pea pods begin twisting open, spilling the seeds.
COLLECTION: Strip the remaining pods off plants after at least 20 percent or so have dried and opened.
PROCESSING: Spread pods on a cookie sheet or board and allow to dry completely. Rub lightly to open remaining pods. Sift through a #4 screen and winnow to remove remaining debris.

MINT, SAWTOOTH MOUNTAIN
Agastache urticifolia (P)
FLOWER: Large pink aromatic groups of flowers. Plant grows 3' tall. Blooms: July to August.
SEED: Dark-brown, watermelon-shaped, 1/16" long. Papery, blond capsules hold seeds quite well until the beginning of winter.
COLLECTION: Begin harvesting entire dried flower when dry and light brown.
PROCESSING: Sift through a #12 or #16 screen. Winnow to remove debris.

PENSTEMON
Few flowers match the brilliance and adaptability of penstemon.
Penstemon cyananthus (P) Wasatch penstemon.
FLOWER: These deep-blue flowers turn purple when mature. Plant grows 2' tall. Blooms: second year, June to July.
P. fruticosus (P) Rock penstemon.
FLOWER: Large lavender blossoms blanket gray-green, low-growing, 10" shrubs. Blooms: first or second year, August to September.

P. palmeri (P) Palmer's penstemon.
FLOWER: Beautiful large pale-pink flowers on tall (4') stems. Blooms: first or second year, August to September.
P. procerus (P) Small-flowered penstemon.
FLOWER: Individual flowers may be small (1/2"), but the overall display is a striking combination of blossoms on stalks 8" to 18" tall. Blooms: 2nd year, June to July.
P. strictus (P) Rocky Mountain penstemon.
FLOWER: Stunning lavender-blue flowers turn deep-purple when mature. Plant grows to 2 1/2' tall. Blooms: second year, July to August.
SEED: Depending on the species, light-brown, hard, raisin-shaped, between 1/16" and 1/8" in length. Once open, the cuplike capsules hold seeds for several weeks. Seed is easily spilled if disturbed by wind or rain.
COLLECTION: Carefully shake mature capsules into an open bag to avoid further cleaning. To collect large amounts, snap off hard, brown capsules and put in a cloth bag.
PROCESSING: Crush unopened capsules with wooden mallet. Sift through a #12 or #16 screen. Winnow to remove remaining debris.

POPPY, CALIFORNIA

Eschscholzia californica (P)
California's state flower. One of the most popular wildflowers.
FLOWER: Brilliant, golden-orange blossoms appear early and remain blooming, often until first snow. Acts as an annual in some unprotected mountain areas. Plant grows 12" to 18" tall. Blooms: July to October.
SEED: Brown, round, 1/16" in diameter. When dry, the long, pointed, 3/4" capsules spill seeds immediately.
COLLECTION: Wait to collect capsules until they begin to turn brown but before they shatter and disperse their seeds.
PROCESSING: Allow capsules to finish drying, then crush to free remaining seeds. Sift through a #12 screen. Winnow to remove remaining debris.

POPPY (SHIRLEY, ICELAND, ORIENTAL)

Papaver rhoeas (A) Flanders or corn poppy.
FLOWER: Brilliant-red to pink, crinkled flowers on slender, hairy stem. Plant grows 18" to 24" tall. Blooms: July to August.
Papaver nudicaule (P) Iceland poppy.
FLOWER: White, pink, yellow, or orange. Translucent crinkled petals top long, hairy stems. Plant grows 1' tall. Blooms: July to August.
Papaver orientale (P) Oriental poppy.
FLOWER: Exceptionally large, orange poppies. Plant grows 3' tall. Blooms: June to early July.
SEED: Cashew-shaped, under 1/16". *P. rhoeas* seeds are light-brown. *P. nudicaule*

and *P. orientale* seeds are black. Closed, cuplike capsules mature with slit-like openings below upper rim. Seeds begin to spill immediately, though some will remain until shaken by wind, rain, or passers-by.

COLLECTION: Snap off capsules when dry and brown but before slits are completely open.

PROCESSING: Allow to dry completely. Shake out remaining seeds. Sift through a #12 or #16 screen.

SHOOTING STAR

Dodecatheon pulchellum (P)

FLOWER: Delicate purple and yellow flowers with reflexed petals. They actually resemble little shooting stars. Plant grows 6" to 18" tall. Blooms: May to June.

SEED: Reddish-brown, blocky-shaped, 1/16". Once open, the cuplike capsules hold seeds for several weeks (if not disturbed by wind or rain).

COLLECTION: Carefully shake mature capsules into an open bag to avoid further cleaning. To collect large amounts of seed, snap off hard, brown capsules.

PROCESSING: Crush unopened capsules in a cloth bag with a wooden mallet. Sift through a #12 screen.

APPENDIXES

APPENDIX A

GLOSSARY

alternate-day caging A technique that allows two different flowering varieties to be pollinated by insects without being cross-pollinated. Cages constructed of wood, wire, or plastic frames are covered with fine screen. One variety is covered with cages one day, allowing the other to be visited and pollinated by insects; the cages are switched each day to allow insect access to the previously caged variety.

anther Organ where pollen is produced.

chaff Broken pieces of dried seed capsules, stems, leaves and other debris mixed in with seeds.

characteristics General features caused by unidentified complexes of genes including but not limited to freeze tolerance, cold tolerance, regional adaptability, winter hardiness, early maturation, and flavor.

cleaning screen Screens with different-sized openings are used to separate seeds from chaff. The screen number denotes the number of openings that will cover a one inch line. A screen is selected with openings just large enough to let seeds drop through without the chaff or as in the case of larger seeds, a screen selected to allow the chaff to drop through without the seeds.

cross-pollination When pollen is exchanged between different flowers from the same or different plants.

dehiscent A seed capsule opened to discharge seeds is dehiscent. Seeds must be harvested before this process takes place and the seeds are lost. In some varieties, the seed capsules literally explode.

dioecious A species with male flowers and female flowers on separate plants.

dominant trait The variation of a specific, identifiable gene that results in observable traits. For example, tall is a dominant trait in pea plant growth. Crosses with bush varieties will usually result in tall varieties. See "trait."

F1 hybrid The "F" in F1 hybrid stands for filial or offspring. F1 means the first generation offspring after controlled pollination between distinct (inbred) parents. Seed saved from F1s lacks the consistency of F1s but can contain desirable traits.

filament Tube that supports the anther where pollen is produced.

flail The process of fracturing or crushing seedpods in order to free the seeds. This can take the form of everything from simply rubbing broccoli pods between your hands to driving over bean vines with a car.

flower The part of a plant where reproduction takes place and seeds are produced.

hybrid Hybrids, the modern definition, are uniform varieties resulting from controlled pollination between distinct (inbred) parents. F1's are the 1st generation offspring after pollination. F2 hybrids, grown from seed saved from F1's, lack the consistency of F1's but usually retain desirable traits that can be stabilized with further selection.

inbreeding depression A loss of vigor because of inbreeding. Inbreeding is the result of self-pollination or pollination between two close relatives.

insect pollination Pollen is carried from one flower to another by insects.

monecious A species is monecious if it produces single plants with separate male flowers and female flowers on the same plant.

open-pollinated Open-pollinated varieties are stable varieties resulting from the uncontrolled pollination between the same or genetically similar parents. Not hybrid.

ovary The female part of a flower that contains the ovules. Fertilized ovules develop into mature seeds.

pappus Small hairs borne at tip of seed (composite flowers only).

perfect flowers Individual flowers that contain both stamens and pistils.

pistil The female reproductive organ in a flower made up of the stigma, style, and ovary.

pollen Equivalent of sperm in plants. Pollen grains fertilize plant ovules.

pollination The process of sexual fertilization in plants. The male chromosomes contained in pollen are combined with the female chromosomes contained in the ovules.

recessive trait The variation of a specific, identifiable gene that results in observable traits only if the dominant trait is not present. For example, wrinkled pea seeds result only in varieties where the dominant smooth-seed trait is not expressed.

rogue The process of removing or destroying plants with unwanted characteristics or traits.

selection The process of saving the seeds from plants that exhibit desirable characteristics and traits.

self-pollination Pollination takes place within a single flower. Other flowers or plants are not needed. Self-pollinating flowers are called "perfect flowers" because they contain the stamens that produce pollen and the pistil that receives the pollen. Isolation distance to prevent cross-pollination is not necessary unless insects are known to invade the flowers before pollination is complete.

silique (siliqua) Long, tube-like seedpod that splits in half.

stamen A flower's male reproductive organ consisting of the filament, anther, and pollen.

stigma The opening in the pistil through which the pollen passes to the ovary.

style Contains the pollen tube between the stigma and the ovary through which the pollen is carried.

thresh A term used by seed professionals to describe the process of separating seeds from chaff.

trait A specific feature traced to an identifiable gene or group of genes. Pea traits traceable to single genes include vine growth (bush or tall), seed texture (smooth or wrinkled) and disease resistance (fusarium, enation mosaic, and powdery mildew).

viable A viable seed is one that will germinate and produce a vigorous plant. Seeds must not be harvested before they have matured enough to be viable. There is wide variation in the point of maturity at which a seed can be harvested and still be viable.

vigor Strong, vibrant germination and growth. A desirable characteristic.

wind pollination When pollen is carried from one flower to another by the wind.

winnow An ancient technique used to clean seeds—moving air from a fan or breeze is used to separate heavier seeds from lighter chaff.

APPENDIX B

BIBLIOGRAPHY

Ashworth, Suzanne. *Seed to Seed: Seed Saving and Growing Techniques for Vegetable Gardeners*, 2nd Edition. Seed Savers Exchange, 2002.

Deppe, Carol. *Breed Your Own Vegetable Varieties: The Gardener's and Farmer's Guide to Plant Breeding and Seed Saving*, 2nd Edition. Chelsea Green, 2000

Fehr, Walter R., and Henry H. Hadley, eds. *Hybridization of Crop Plants*. American Society of Agronomy and Crop Science Society of Am, 1980. Revised 1982.

Fowler, Cary, and Mooney, Pat. *Shattering: Food, Politics, And The Loss of Genetic Diversity*. Tucson, Arizona: U of Arizona Press, 1990. Ganders, Fred R.

Griffiths, Anthony J. F. *Wildflower Genetics*. Flight, 1983.

Johnston, Robert, Jr. *Growing Garden Seeds*, Johnnys Selected Seeds. 2nd ed. 1983.

Navazio, John, *The Organic Seed Grower: A Farmer's Guide to Vegetable Seed Production*. Chelsea Green Publishing, 2012

Welsh, James R. *Fundamentals of Plant Genetics and Breeding*. Wiley, 1981.

Young, James A. and Cheryl G. *Seeds of Wildland Plants: Collecting, Processing and Germinating*. Timber Press, 1986

Zystro, Jared and Colley, Micaela *The Seed Garden: The Art and Practice of Seed Saving*. Decorah, Iowa: Seed Savers Exchange, 2015

APPENDIX C

SOURCES

SEED SAVING EQUIPMENT

Pollination Bags: Lawson Bag Company, PO Box 8577, Northfield, IL 60093. http://www.lawsonbags.com/

Cleaning Screens: Jesse DeMoss, 3348 Walker Ln., New Meadows, ID 83654 jessedemoss@hotmail.com

Cleaning Equipment: Hoffman Manufacturing, Inc., 16541 Green Bridge Road, Jefferson, OR 97352-9201, Phone: 800-692-5962, http://www.hoffmanmfg.com/

MY FAVORITE OPEN-POLLINATED SEED COMPANIES

All Good Things Organic Seeds, plantgoodseed.com, Ojai, CA
Aravaipa Heirlooms, aravaipa.com, Oracle, AZ
Brim Seed Co., brimseed.com, Ross, TX
Family Farmers Seed Co-op, organicseedcoop.com, Boone, CO
Fertile Valley Seeds, caroldeppe.com, Corvallis, OR
Free Wild Seed, freewildseed.com, NY
Foundroot Seeds, Sundries & Sustenance, foundroot.com, Palmer, AK
Good Seed Company, goodseedco.net, Whitefish, MT
Heritage Grain Conservancy, growseed.org, Colrain, MA
Landrace Seedlist, garden.lofthouse.com/seed-list.phtml, Paradise, UT
Miss Penn's Mountain Seeds, pennandcordsgarden.com, Westcliffe, CO
The Living Seed Company, livingseedcompany.com, Point Reyes Station, CA
Seeds Trust, High Altitude Gardens, seedstrust.com, Littleton, CO
Sierra Seeds, sierraseeds.org, North San Juan, CA
Siskiyou Seeds, siskiyouseeds.com, Williams, OR
Snake River Seed Coop, snakeriverseeds.com, Boise, ID
Urban Tomato, urbantomato.ca, Peterborough, ONT, Canada

SEED SCHOOL

(1 and 6 day intensives and online webinars)
Seedsave.org, PO Box 596, Cornville, AZ 86325 belle@seedsave.org

CONNECT

Facebook: https://www.facebook.com/seedsave.org/
Twitter: @billmcdorman

APPENDIX D

INDEX

seeds 7
  cleaning equipment 40
  collecting
    wildflower 25
    ecologically sensitive 25
  storage bags 40
seed to seed 8
selection 8, 38
  characteristics 9, 37
  trait 9, 39
self-incompatible 7
self-pollination 7, 38
separation distance 8
SHOOTING STAR 36
silique (siliqua) 38
SPINACH 17
Spinacia oleracae 17
SQUASH 18
stamen 7, 39
  anther 7, 37
  filament 7, 38
  pollen 7, 38
stigma 7, 39
storage 10
style 7, 39
SWISS CHARD 19

T

tagging 26
thresh 9, 39
timing 26
TOMATO 13
trait 9, 39
  dominant 9, 37
  recessive 38
TURNIP 23

V

viable 9, 39
vigor 8, 39

W

wind pollination 39
winnow 9, 39
WITLOOF CHICORY 22

X

Xerophyllum tenax 28

Z

Zea mays 15